I GOT IT FROM MY MAMA! GREGOR MENDEL EXPLAINS HEREDITY

Science Book Age 9
Children's Biology Books

BABY PROFESSOR

EDUCATION KIDS

Speedy Publishing LLC

40 E. Main St. #1156

Newark, DE 19711

www.speedypublishing.com

Copyright 2017

Why do kids so often look like their parents? And why do they sometimes look different? How people, animals, and plants inherit their traits is a mystery that Gregor Mendel helped to solve. Let's find out how!

THE MYSTERY OF HEREDITY

For centuries farmers have known that, in general, if you have a plant and use seeds from it, the resulting plants will look and act much like the plant you got the seeds from and the plant that fertilized the seeds. That's why farmers try to combine the best plants: so they can improve the harvest in future years.

They have also known that if you cross-fertilize plants with a related plant, one result may be a stronger and more productive plant. However, nobody really understood how this worked, or how you could predict results.

Gregor Mendel

Gregor Mendel lived in Moravia, now part of the Czech Republic, from 1822 to 1884. He was a monk and a scientist, and worked to understand the process by which offspring inherit traits from their parents. His studies laid the groundwork for understanding genetics and heredity.

GREGOR MENDEL AT WORK

As a young man, Mendel worked on the family farm tending bees and gardening. He often had to interrupt his studies because of illness and poverty. He became a monk partly so that he could complete his education for free. He taught high school and did research, on top of his religious duties. He was not a great student, and he did not perform very well in exams, but he still went on to make many discoveries as a result of patient work over many years.

Gregor Mendel among his fellow monks

Mendel published papers on bees and astronomy and meteorology, and most of his surviving published papers are about weather patterns.

Several of Mendel's teachers were conducting studies in animal development, and encouraged Mendel to look at how traits are handed on from generation to generation. Mendel concentrated on plants instead of animals, and got the use of several acres of an experimental farm for his work.

EXPERIMENTS WITH PEA PLANTS

Mendel decided to work with pea plants because he could grow two generations each year. This would make it easier to collect data about how traits are passed on than it is when working with animals, whose period between their birth and when they can have their own children is longer—often much longer.

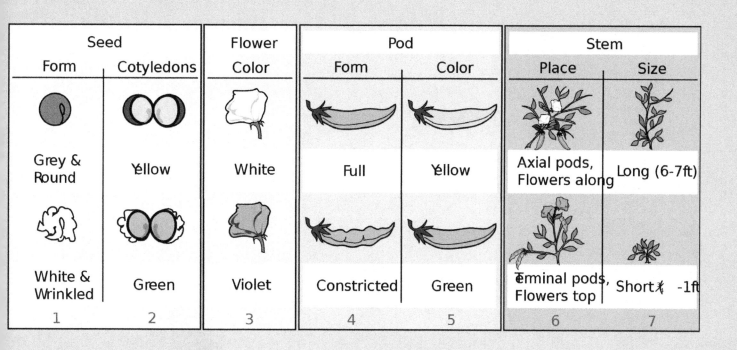

Seed		Flower	Pod		Stem	
Form	Cotyledons	Color	Form	Color	Place	Size
Grey & Round	Yellow	White	Full	Yellow	Axial pods, Flowers along	Long (6-7ft)
White & Wrinkled	Green	Violet	Constricted	Green	Terminal pods, Flowers top	Short ½ -1ft
1	2	3	4	5	6	7

7 Characteristics of a Pea Plant

Mendel also studied bees and mice, but his superior in the religious order did not like his research using animals. Also, the bees were very aggressive and kept stinging the other monks so Mendel, who was very fond of the bees, had to get rid of them.

There were a number of traits in pea plants that seemed to Mendel to be worth looking at. He wanted to see how the offspring inherited the parent plants' height, seed shape, seed color, flower color, flower location, pod shape, the color of the unripe pod and flower location. He started with seed shape, which was either round or angular.

Green Pea Plant

Gregor Mendel 1822-1884

From 1856 to 1863 Mendel grew and studied about 28,000 plants. He began to understand the nature of dominant and recessive inheritance.

DOMINANT AND RECESSIVE

Neither Mendel, nor anybody else at the time, understood all the details of how cells pass on their features. He did not know what we now know about genes and DNA, but he could observe among his peas that there was a pattern in the way traits are passed on.

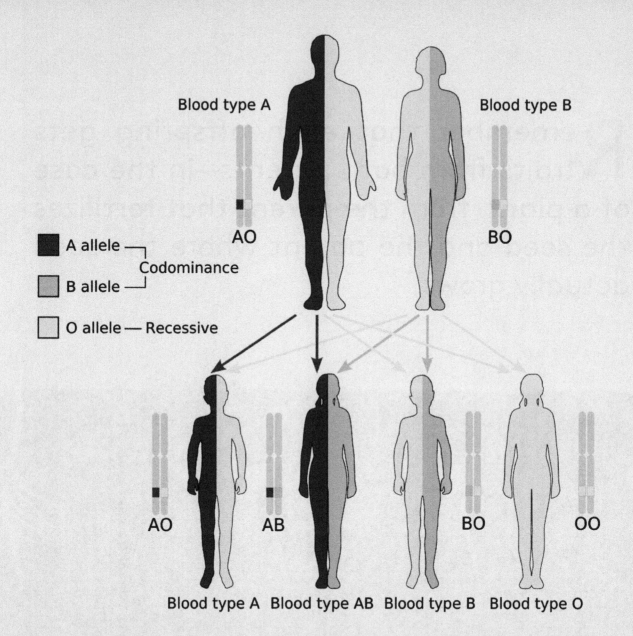

Blood type A

Blood type B

A allele ┐
          ├ Codominance
B allele ┘

O allele — Recessive

AO

BO

AO

AB

BO

OO

Blood type A   Blood type AB   Blood type B   Blood type O

Mendelian Traits in Humans

Remember that each offspring gets traits from both parents—in the case of a plant, from the parent that fertilizes the seed and the parent where the seed actually grows.

L et's make up a plant that has a trait that the leaves will be either round (r) or pointy (p). The new plant gets one instruction about leaf shape from one parent, and another from the other parent. So the new plant could get any one of three instruction pairs: r+r, r+p or p+p.

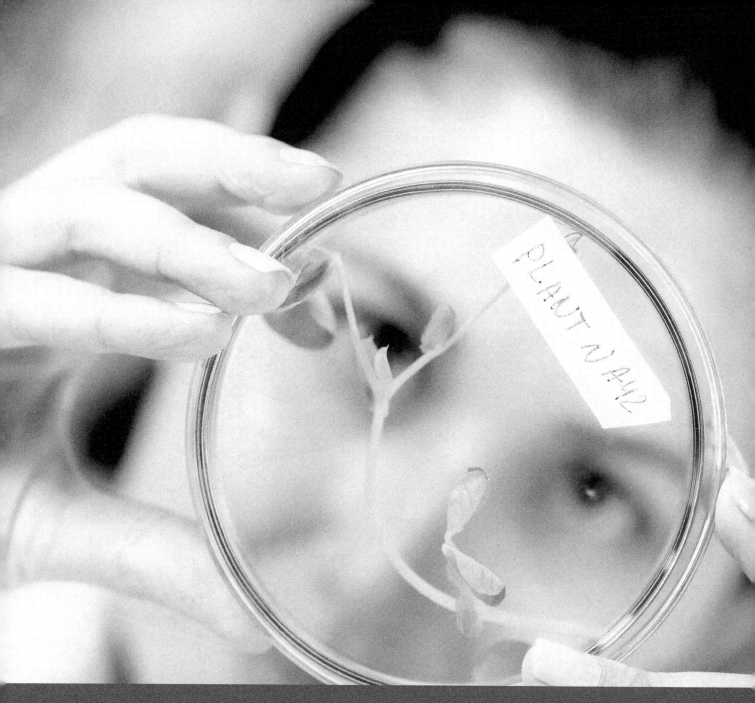

A woman checking the progress of an experiment.

It's pretty clear that if the new plant gets an r+r instruction, its leaves will tend to be round, and if it gets p+p, its leaves will tend to be pointy. But what happens to the new plants that get a mixed r+p instruction? If you found that the new plants with r+p tended to

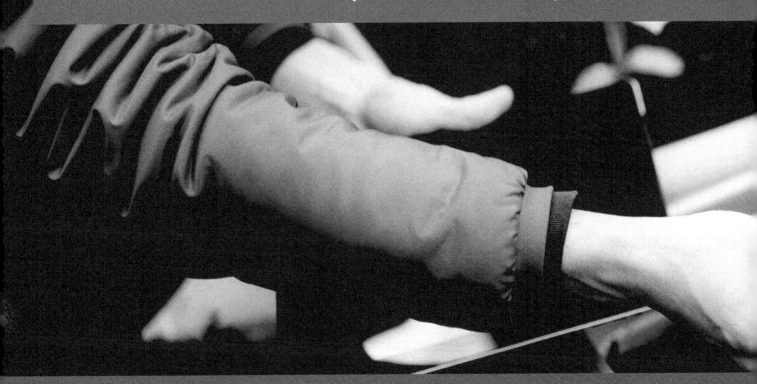

Checking the pointy and rounded leaves

grow rounded leaves, you would say that the r instruction is dominant and the p instruction is recessive. If the new plants tended to grow pointy leaves, you would say that p was the dominant instruction and r was recessive.

Remember that inheritance is not like a light switch, which is either on or off. A lot more goes into inheriting traits than this simple example can illustrate. But this is a start at understanding what Mendel discovered.

MENDEL'S THREE DISCOVERIES

From what he saw among the pea plants, Mendel proposed three laws:

1. The Law of Segregation

2. The Law of Independent Assortment

3. The Law of Dominance

Experiments on Plants

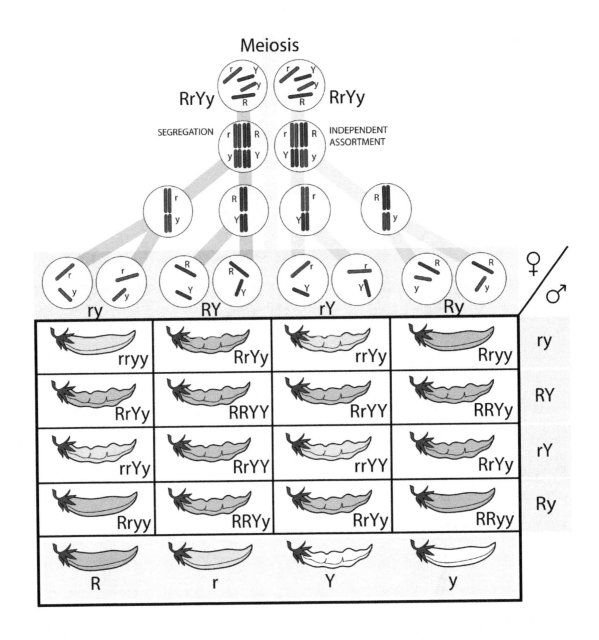

Independent assortment & segregation

The Law of Segregation

This law states that genes are in pairs (p+p, p+r or r+r in our simple example) and that each parent passes on to its offspring only one half of that pair. So, for a parent with a p+r leaf instruction, it could pass on either the p or the r part. That half of the instruction joins with the half the other parent provided to provide a gene pair for the offspring.

The Law of Independent Assortment

The Law of Independent Assortment states that trait information is independent of information about other traits. If the parent pea plant is passing on instructions about seed shape and seed color, for instance, the half of the instruction pair that it passes on for seed shape is independent from the half that it passes on for seed color.

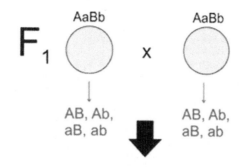

F₂	AB	Ab	aB	ab
AB	AABB	AABb	AaBB	AaBb
Ab	AABb	AAbb	AaBb	Aabb
aB	AaBB	AaBb	aaBB	aaBb
ab	AaBb	Aabb	aaBb	aabb

9 ⬤ : 3 🌼 : 3 ⬤ : 1 🌼

Mendel's law of independent assortment

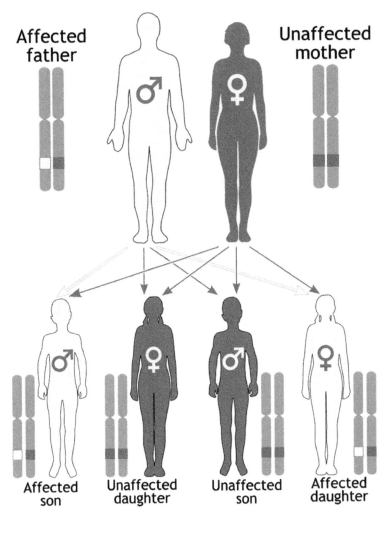

Affected father

Unaffected mother

Affected son

Unaffected daughter

Unaffected son

Affected daughter

■ Unaffected
□ Affected

Autosomal Dominant

The Law of Dominance

To go back to our simple example, if the child plant receives the mixed instruction p+r about leaf shape, and if p is the dominant trait, then the child plant's leaves will tend to be pointy.

M endel bred together plants with yellow peas and plants with green peas. He found that the next generation of plants produced all yellow peas, but that in the generation after that about one quarter of the plants produced peas that were green.

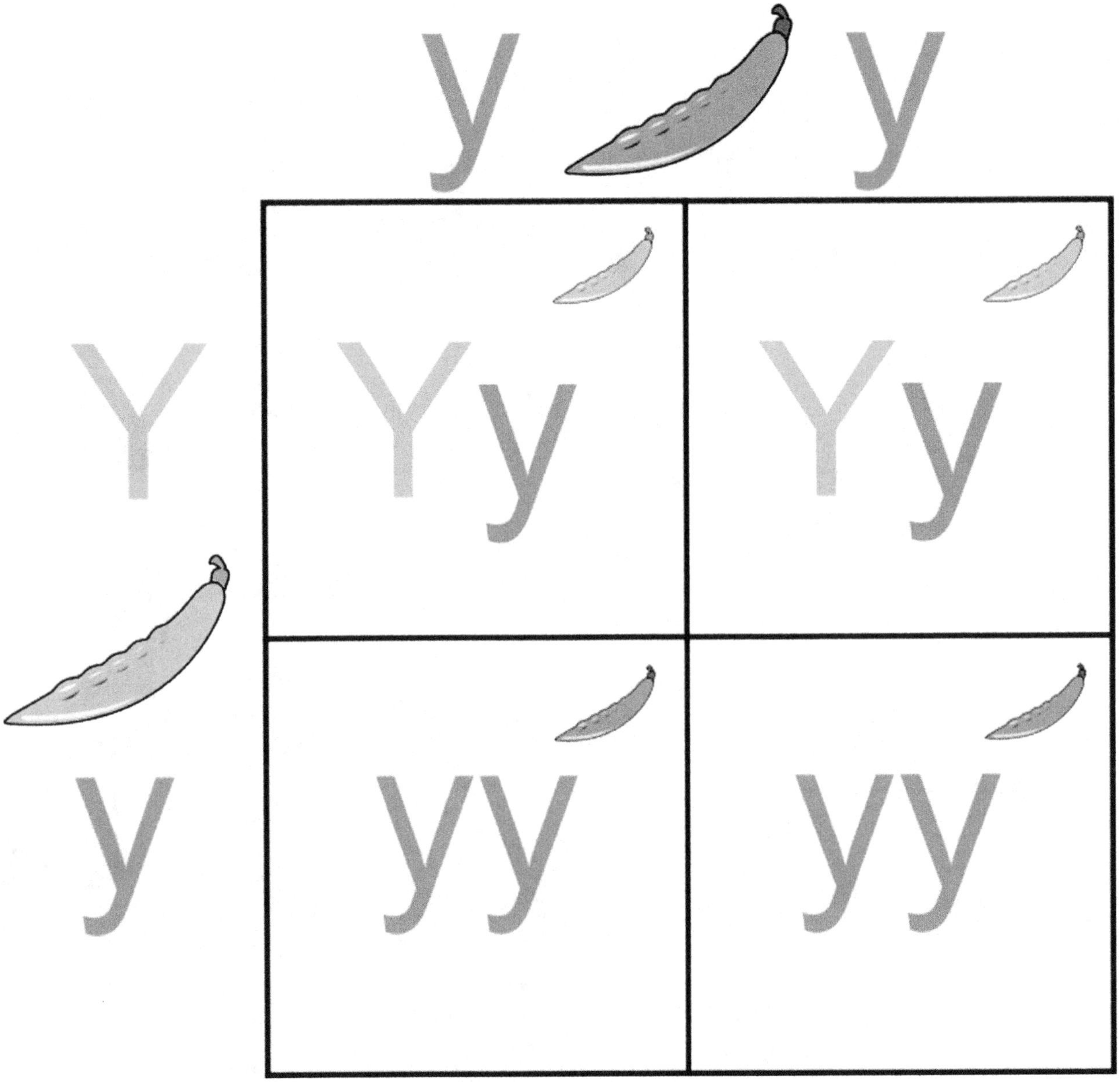

y
y
Y
y
Yy
Yy
yy
yy

He concluded that the gene for the color yellow was dominant over the gene for the color green, but that a quarter of the time the new plant received two recessive "green" instructions from its parents.

These laws are now known as Mendel's Laws of Inheritance.

MENDEL'S INFLUENCE

Mendel published the results of his studies in 1865, and in general the scientific community rejected them. This was partly because Mendel was not a university professor with lots of titles, and partly because what he found ran against the general understanding at the time about inheritance.

Gregor Mendel Statue in Brno, Czech Republic

At the time, people thought that the parents' genetic material was sort of blended together, so that the offspring received everything from both parents in a new mixture. Mendel's Laws ran against this understanding.

Mendel's church responsibilities took more and more of his time, and he had less time for research. He became abbot, the head of his monastery, in 1868, and spent a lot of time in administration and in legal disputes between the monastery and local governments over taxes.

reason... ...t deal of speculation has gone into does a ...he
Navid... ...avidson chose to resume the lesson. ...lit ...a ...he
years... ...elf never deals with... specifically and which a...
three s...

I. The Kellog-Antwerk Claim

...]. The Bister Frieght-Josephsof Criteria

...III. The Haven Slocum Theory

...to address all their respective n...
...ven to their views. 55a

...ernment of In...

Steve Wozniak.

Woz: I like Ross' idea. A giant chip. Or a s...
All interconnected. If only I could see the...
could tell you if it's for something sexy o...
hardware— like a cosmic toaster or blender.

...ley Kubrick.

Kubrick: I'm sorry. I've said enough.

Leslie Stern, M.D.

Stern: More importantly Karen, what d...

[End Of Tra

331So many voices. Not that I'm un...
opinion, need and compulsion but...

Thumper just called (henc...
A welcome voice.
Strange how th...
...se cal...

After his death in 1884, the new abbot burned most of Mendel's papers, including his research notes and letters. This was mainly to get rid of material related to various tax disputes that had now been settled. Nobody realized that his research materials would have been useful to future scientists.

Mendel's discoveries were mostly forgotten until 1900, long after Mendel had died. In that year two researchers independently published papers about inheritance that confirmed what Mendel had proposed in his Laws. One of them, Hugo de Vries, could not make sense of his research findings until he happened to read Mendel's paper from 35 years previously.

Hugo de Vries

S ome twentieth-century scientists doubted Mendel's results, and felt he must have made them up or changed them to fit what he wanted to see. This is known as "**confirmation bias**". However, other researchers have duplicated

Mendel's experiments and have found no reason to think that Mendel was not reporting accurately what he saw among his pea plants.

By the 1930s and 1940s, scientists were combining Mendel's insights with Charles Darwin's theories of natural selection, and the discoveries of other researchers, to develop the modern science of genetics and the modern understanding of inheritance and heredity.

Charles Darwin

HEREDITY AFFECTS US ALL

Who you are in part depends on what you inherit from your parents. In that, you are very like one of Mendel's pea plants! Of course, the resources and opportunities you have, and what you do with what you inherited, combine with your genetic materials to make the interesting person that you are.

Understanding heredity helps us to understand how life develops and how new species come to be, but it is just one part of the puzzle of life on Earth.

Read more Baby Professor books, like Where did You Get the Color of Your Eyes?, to understand more!

Visit

BABY PROFESSOR
EDUCATION KIDS

www.BabyProfessorBooks.com

to download Free Baby Professor eBooks
and view our catalog of new and exciting
Children's Books

Made in the USA
Middletown, DE
11 November 2018